This book belongs to:

____

Made in the USA
Las Vegas, NV
22 April 2022

47848030R00069